MODERN ROLE MODELS

Miley Cyrus

David Robson

Mason Crest Publishers

Produced by OTTN Publishing in association with
21st Century Publishing and Communications, Inc.

MASON CREST PUBLISHERS INC.
370 Reed Road
Broomall, Pennsylvania 19008
(866) MCP-BOOK (toll free)
www.masoncrest.com

Printed in the United States of America.

9 8 7 6 5 4 3 2

Library of Congress Cataloging-in-Publication Data

Robson, David, 1966–
    Miley Cyrus / David Robson.
       p. cm. — (Modern role models)
ISBN-13: 978-1-4222-0501-3 (hardcover) — ISBN-13: 978-1-4222-0788-8 (pbk.)
 1. Cyrus, Miley, 1992–   —Juvenile literature. 2. Singers—United States—
Biography—Juvenile literature. 3. Actresses—United States—Biography—
Juvenile literature. I. Title.
ML3930.C98R63 2008
782.42164092—dc22
[B]   2008020402

Publisher's note:
All quotations in this book come from original sources, and contain the spelling
and grammatical inconsistencies of the original text.

CROSS-CURRENTS

*In the ebb and flow of the currents of life we are each influenced
by many people, places, and events that we directly experience
or have learned about. Throughout the chapters of this book you
will come across CROSS-CURRENTS reference boxes. These
boxes direct you to a CROSS-CURRENTS section in the back
of the book that contains fascinating and informative sidebars
and related pictures. Go on.* ▸▸

CONTENTS

Miley Cyrus performs as Hannah Montana during a stop on the Best of Both Worlds Tour, 2008. To her legions of young fans, Miley combines the glamour of a rock star with the down-to-earth appeal of the girl next door. This blend has made the teenager one of today's hottest pop stars.

1

The Best

THE LIGHTS DIM AND THE VOICES OF 20,000 young girls rise to a scream, threatening to blow the roof off of the packed arena. They have waited months for this—a chance to see their idol up close. The anticipation in the air is electric; they will not have to wait long now.

Out of the darkness, the music thumps, then the stage lights flash, and with a roar from the crowd Hannah Montana takes the stage. Her shoulder-length blonde locks bob to the beat of the drums; she stands center stage and belts out the words to "Rock Star":

> **"**I could fix the flat on your car/I might even be a . . . rock star/If you only knew the real me/I might even be a rock star.**"**

Despite the lyrics, Hannah Montana's **throngs** of young admirers already feel like they know the real her. They know that Hannah

Montana is only a television character played by 15-year-old Miley Ray Cyrus. Wearing a wig to cover her long brown hair, Miley is not fooling anybody. Her double life is an open secret, but her admirers play along. That is part of the fun. They line up in all sorts of weather for concert tickets and dress themselves in Hannah Montana shirts, wear Hannah Montana lipstick, and carry Hannah Montana hand-bags. They cannot get enough. Excited fans like Meghan and Brooke even post their once-in-a-lifetime experiences on the Internet:

> **"We rocked out to every single song, shaked half to death, and screamed at the top of our lungs when Hannah came out of her pink box, and almost cried when Miley said that the finale was happening. We belted our hearts out to the last song, 'Best of Both Worlds,' and after hurried to go beat the souvenir lines. "**

According to millions of girls across the nation and the world, Miley Cyrus is, indeed, the real thing. Sure, Miley might look like the girl next door—she's likable and down-to-earth—but the smiley brunette with impeccable comic timing is, instead, the biggest pop star of her generation. Miley's television show, *Hannah Montana*, is a monster hit; her first three albums have sold millions of copies; and she regularly walks red carpets wearing glamorous dresses and waving to her **legions** of fans.

CROSS-CURRENTS

To find out how Miley shows her compassion for others, read "Extreme Miley: A Chance to Give Back." Go to page 48. ▶▶

⟩⟩ UP AND AWAY ⟨⟨

Miley's rise to superstardom has surprised even the most **jaded** Hollywood executives. *Hannah Montana* debuted in March 2006 on the Disney Channel before a showing of the popular movie *High School Musical.* Almost immediately, it became one of the most highly rated shows in the country. The weekly adventures of Miley Stewart and her quirky but lovable family quickly propelled the young star beyond ordinary popularity and into the pop culture stratosphere.

Miley had banner years in 2007 and early 2008, with hundreds of personal appearances and armfuls of awards. At the 2008 Nickelodeon's Kids' Choice Awards, the audience chanted for her:

"Miley, Miley!" When the category of "Favorite TV Actress" was announced, the envelope ripped open and her name was finally read, Miley rushed to the stage and tried to look surprised. But this was no surprise. It was Miley's year.

Miley's 2007–2008 Best of Both Worlds Tour was a huge success, earning more than $36 million in ticket sales. All 69 of Miley's shows sold out quickly—some in as little as five minutes, according to media reports! The difficulty of getting tickets to the live performances disappointed many of Miley's fans.

Before the Teen Choice Awards ceremony, a smiling Miley poses with a surfboard. She won a pair of awards at the August 2007 presentation: "Choice Summer Artist" and "Choice TV Actress in a Comedy." Earlier in the year, Miley had won a Kids' Choice Awards as "Favorite TV Actress," showing her popularity among young people.

Beginning in late 2007, Miley toured the country as fictional pop star Hannah Montana. In the past, she had played second fiddle to other, more popular acts, such as the Cheetah Girls. But long box-office lines, which led to jam-packed stadiums and concert halls, proved that Miley had come into her own; she was flying solo. With a tight band, and some assistance from opening act the Jonas Brothers, she took the music world by storm.

Those fans disappointed at not being able to get tickets to see Miley live were given a second chance. In early 2008 the **three-dimensional** (3D) concert movie *Hannah Montana and Miley Cyrus: Best of Both Worlds Concert* played at movie houses from Maine to California, becoming the country's number-one box-office sensation. Yet Miley Cyrus's enormous success was by no means certain, although her early life and family story might make it seem that way.

CROSS-CURRENTS

3-D movies are nothing new; they were first created in the 1890s. To learn more, read "Reaching Out: Miley in 3-D." Go to page 49. ▶▶

⟩⟩ DESTINED ⟨⟨

Born into a show business family near Nashville, Tennessee, Miley Cyrus, it seems, was destined for the **limelight**. Her father, after all, made his name in the early 1990s with a toe-tapping, chart-topping country hit. Still, despite the family history, fame and fortune did not come so easily to Miley. Overnight sensations are often years in the making, and it was no different for Miley. She spent countless hours reading, rehearsing, auditioning, and waiting for the big break she dreamed would come. But, once the fuse on Miley's career was lit, it was only a matter of time before it exploded.

Today, Miley Cyrus stands near the top of the entertainment heap. For a person so young to have reached so high in so brief a time is nothing short of astounding. If destiny is hard work combined with a pinch of luck, Miley may just be the luckiest teenager in the world, and she knows it:

> **❝I've always loved singing, and I've always loved acting and dancing. Getting this opportunity with Disney, I get to do it all. They let you do everything you love.❞**

Country singer Billy Ray Cyrus holds his infant daughter while performing a concert in the mid-1990s. Billy Ray became a huge singing star, selling millions of albums, after his song "Achy Breaky Heart" hit number one on the country charts in 1992. To support his albums, Billy Ray toured the United States throughout the 1990s.

2

Smiley

MILEY WAS BORN DESTINY HOPE CYRUS IN Franklin, Tennessee, on November 23, 1992. Her father, Billy Ray, and her mother, Tish, chose that name because they thought their daughter's destiny would be to bring the world hope. That might sound like a tall order for a newborn, especially since at the time it was Billy Ray who was riding high.

Billy Ray Cyrus had once dreamed of playing professional baseball, but he could also play a mean guitar and write songs. After many years of struggle, his hard work finally paid off just about the time tiny Destiny came along. Billy Ray—sporting a stylish haircut—scored his first big hit in 1992 with "Achy Breaky Heart," a catchy country tune that propelled him to the top of the music charts.

Despite his newfound celebrity and almost constant touring, Billy Ray was a dedicated family man. And what a large family his was becoming. Aside from Destiny, the Cyrus clan included her half-brothers, Christopher Cody and Trace, and her half-sister, Brandi. In spite of

CROSS-CURRENTS

If you'd like to find out more about Billy Ray Cyrus's life and early career, check out "Achy-Breaky Pop." Go to page 50. ▶▶

the challenges, Billy Ray and Tish were committed to keeping the family together as much as possible. That often meant bringing the growing **brood** on tour.

On the road, Billy Ray and Tish immediately noticed their youngest daughter's sunny disposition. Their child was always grinning from ear to ear. Thus, Tish and Billy Ray gave their new baby a nickname: Smiley. Young Destiny, with her curly brown locks, could not pronounce the name herself. So "Smiley" became "Miley." The name stuck.

⇒ GROWING FAMILY ⇐

When off the road and back at home in Franklin, the Cyruses worked to give Miley and her siblings as stable a home life as possible. The family also grew at this time: new brother, Braison, was born on May 9, 1994. Six years later, on January 8, 2000, Miley's sister Noah came along.

Miley and her siblings got lots of play time to develop their self-confidence and have fun. Still, early on it became clear that Miley had inherited the performing **gene** from her dad. She later said,

> **"When I was little, I would stand up on couches and say 'Watch me!' We had these showers that are completely glass, and I would lock people in them and make them stay in there and watch me perform. I'd make them watch."**

Although her family saw her as a natural performer, few people outside her home knew how badly Miley wanted a chance at stardom. However, it would not be long before the family secret became public knowledge.

⇒ THE BIG MOVE ⇐

In 2001 life changed dramatically for the Cyrus family. Billy Ray was hired to star in the new television series *Doc*. If the family was to remain together, it would have to move to Toronto, Canada, hundreds of miles from its beloved Tennessee. It was not an easy decision; leaving home never is. Billy Ray's music career had taken off in Tennessee, a state known for its glorious musical heritage. Nashville is the unofficial capital of the country music industry.

Billy Ray and Tish Cyrus wanted to give their growing family a stable home in Tennessee, but also wanted to be together as much as possible when Billy Ray was on the road. Miley is on the right in this photo of the family taken during one of Billy Ray's concert tours.

Memphis, in the west, is famous for Beale Street, where blues musicians from all over the world come and ply their trade. Elvis Presley, the "King of Rock and Roll," lived in Memphis for much of his life.

But despite the pull of home, the Cyrus family took the leap. *Doc* was a chance for Billy Ray to give acting a real chance, and he made the most of it. In many ways, *Doc* seemed custom-made for Billy Ray Cyrus. On the show, he played Dr. Clint "Doc" Cassidy, a physician

CROSS-CURRENTS

Miley grew up near Nashville, Tennessee. For more information about the city, read "The Home of Country Music." Go to page 51. ▶▶

Young Miley in the front seat of her dad's pickup truck. When an offer came for Billy Ray Cyrus to star in a television show, the family moved to Toronto. It turned out to be a good move, as his show, *Doc*, soon became the highest-rated show on the PAX-TV network.

who moves from the mountains of Montana to the Big Apple, New York City. Doc is a fish out of water, but his Christian values and genuine kindness make him friends and win him the respect of his new community and the clinic in which he works. He shows big-city folk that a country boy has much to teach them. The gentle warmth and humor of the show kept it running on the PAX-TV network from 2001 until 2004.

Miley, meanwhile, was growing up before her parents' eyes. In 2002, with Billy Ray and Tish's encouragement, she appeared on *Doc* as a girl named Kylie. A talent scout must have liked what she saw because she cast 11-year-old Miley in a small role in director Tim Burton's 2003 movie *Big Fish*. That same year, Miley was featured in singer Rhonda Vincent's "If Heartaches Have Wings" music video.

Billy Ray, for one, was not so surprised by his daughter's **ambition** and talent. In fact, he had first witnessed Miley's competitive nature years before:

> **❝Since she was little, she would look at me confidently and say, 'I'm going to blow by you, Daddy. I'm going to be a singer, songwriter, and entertainer.' She was born with a song. Musically, she's the real deal. . . . You know that saying she's got an old soul? Well, she's got an old soul, and her old soul's got a lot of soul.❞**

In 2004, the final season of *Doc*, the old soul was given a larger role on one episode. She played the school friend of a boy named Raul. By now, she had caught the acting bug. While Miley had always been a performer—singing with her dad, dancing around the house with her brothers and sisters—she began taking music and performing more seriously. There seemed to be no stopping her.

Twelve-year-old Miley is all smiles as she poses with her parents and the Pink Sparkle guitar that they have just given her. Miley was soon hired as a spokesperson for Daisy Rock Guitars, which makes instruments for girls and women. She had no way of knowing that even bigger things were just around the corner.

3

The Big Audition

PART OF MILEY'S NEWFOUND FOCUS INCLUDED her determination to **audition** for more acting parts. One of the biggest entertainment companies on the planet, Disney, had its own television channel and regularly cast people Miley's age. Thus, at the tender age of eleven, Miley convinced Billy Ray and Tish to send Disney a videotape of her acting.

Miley was interested in trying out for one of the many television shows broadcast on the Disney Channel. She was confident: by now, she had some acting credits on her **résumé**, and she was sure that her charm and humor would come through on the tape. But after taking a look at Miley's audition, Disney Channel president Gary Marsh took a pass. While he immediately noticed her easy manner in front of the camera, as well as her winning personality, he felt Miley was too small and too inexperienced for any of the roles he was casting. In the "don't call us, we'll call you" world of auditions and rejections,

Miley seemed like just another talented but less than extraordinary kid. The call Miley was waiting for never came.

Miley was terribly disappointed, but still confident in her abilities. She moved on to other projects, refusing to give up her dream of stardom. Miley's persistence began paying dividends quickly. In 2004, as a still-unknown 12-year-old, she signed on as a **spokesperson** for Daisy Rock Guitars. Her first guitar, called a Pink Sparkle, was a gift from her parents. Billy Ray presented it to her during an appearance in front of thousands of people. Maybe this spokesperson contract was a sign that she was destined for something bigger. Little did she know that her time to shine was just around the corner.

By this time the Cyrus family had moved back to their farm in Franklin. Miley spent her days attending middle school and going to local commercial auditions whenever she could find the time. She had no way of knowing, however, that Disney's Gary Marsh was having second thoughts about her. Disney was developing a new show about a regular girl who leads a double life as a platinum-haired pop star named Hannah Montana. After holding hundreds of auditions, Marsh had yet to find his Hannah. One old audition tape kept nagging at him. He sat in his office watching it again and again. He could not quite put a finger on it, but the bubbly girl on the tape had a special sparkle in her eyes and an ability to hold a viewer's attention that few other young actors could match. Marsh had a **hunch**.

Six months after first seeing her, Marsh placed a call to Miley Cyrus in Franklin, Tennessee. He was eager to see if the tiny girl had grown any and whether she might be the missing ingredient for his new show. But before he could make a decision, he would have to meet her face to face. That meant flying Miley and her father to Hollywood for a live audition. Time would tell Marsh whether his hunch was right.

⇒ "LIFE IS WHAT YOU MAKE IT" ⇐

The Disney Company is legendary for finding ways to showcase new talent. Started by **illustrator** Walt Disney in the mid-1920s, the company initially specialized in animated films. Many of these starred Disney's Mickey Mouse, who first appeared in the black-and-white short *Steamboat Willie* in 1928. Almost a decade later, in 1937, came the first feature-length animated film, *Snow White*.

Miley is flanked by Mickey and Minnie Mouse during a visit to Disneyland. Disney Channel executive Gary Marsh liked what he saw of Miley's first audition tape, so in 2004 Marsh asked her to come back for a second audition. Marsh was interested in casting the young actor in the lead role on a new Disney Channel series.

It was an enormous hit and ushered in a golden age of animated successors such as *Sleeping Beauty*, *Cinderella*, and *Fantasia*.

As the company grew, though, live-action movies became an important part of Disney's business plan. In the 1950s and early 1960s, the "House that Walt built" began centering family-friendly films around squeaky-clean tween stars, including Hayley Mills and Annette Funicello. Male stars like Kurt Russell and Dean Jones

CROSS-CURRENTS

To read about some other Disney performers who became big stars, check out "Disney's Star Machine: Hayley Mills and Annette Funicello." Go to page 52. ▶▶

became Disney movie regulars too, attracting teenagers to the movie theaters at a time when television was king.

A more recent Disney star who became famous for both her acting and her singing was Hilary Duff. Miley wanted that kind of versatile career. Now she had a chance to show her stuff.

But although Miley had auditioned for smaller television roles in the past, this audition would be different. It was for a starring role. Would she be able to handle the pressure and win the role of Hannah Montana?

Hayley Mills, who starred in many films during the 1960s and early 1970s, was a famous Disney child star. One of Hayley's most famous roles was in *Pollyanna* (1960). She won a special Academy Award for that film. Another big hit was *The Parent Trap* (1961), in which she played two characters—twin sisters who had been separated as babies.

As the big day approached, Miley had serious work to do. Like most performers trying out for acting roles, Miley memorized a set of lines known as "sides." Upon arriving for the biggest day of her life, she was ushered into a small audition room. She had grown since the Disney executives had first gotten a look at her. She was 12 now—soon to be a teenager—and her confidence was evident to all. Then, with the cameras rolling and an off-screen helper feeding her cue lines, Miley stood and delivered a scene from the script. Marsh saw something special:

> **"We saw a girl who has this natural ebullience. She loves every minute of her life. It shows in her demeanor and performance."**

She got the part. Marsh later said that Miley's comic timing was one reason she was chosen. This refers to the humorous way she could deliver her lines. (Some **critics** would later compare Miley to a legendary television comedian, Lucille Ball). Marsh also appreciated her sweet singing voice. Billy Ray was not surprised at his daughter's good fortune:

> **"As I read the script, I knew it wasn't going to proceed without Miley. It was just one of those inner voice things you feel inside. Six or eight months later, Disney calls back and says 'We'd like to take another look at that Cyrus kid,' and she flew back out to California."**

➤ DADDY'S SURPRISE ◄

What Billy Ray could not have known at that moment was that he would soon be joining Miley for the ride of a lifetime. When he tagged along with her to audition for *Hannah Montana*, he learned that Disney was also casting for Hannah Montana's father. Billy Ray asked to be considered. How funny would it be, he thought, to play your own daughter's father on television.

But after the audition he was sure he was wrong for the part. As written, Hannah's father did not seem to suit the quiet, humble, guitar-slinging country singer. Billy Ray was also reluctant to ruin things for his little girl:

Miley and her father have said that they have a very close relationship. This bond was obvious during their audition, so the country singer was offered the role of Robby Ray Stewart, Miley's father on *Hannah Montana*. According to the show, Robby Ray is a former singer who gave up his career to take care of his children.

> **"I didn't know if I was right for her dad. The last thing I would want to do is screw up Miley's show."**

Yet during their audition, something clicked. Miley had already read with scores of other middle-aged "daddies," but the natural ease and sweetness between parent and child won the day and won Billy Ray the part. Even his own reluctance took a back seat when given the chance to work with his daughter nearly every day. But neither Billy Ray nor Miley could know that their Disney television show would soon become a national phenomenon.

⇒ MAKING IT WORK ⇐

Every year the Disney Channel rolls out a handful of new shows that it hopes will appeal to teens and even younger kids. The term *tween* refers to children old enough to enjoy Disney's brand of wholesome entertainment, but young enough to go crazy over the merchandise connected with its products. Shows like *The Wizards of Waverly Place*, *Cory in the House*, and *The Suite Life of Zack and Cody* sometimes take years to develop and bring to the small screen.

By the time Miley Cyrus was cast as Hannah Montana, the show's basic premise was set. A perky but average middle-school girl lives a secret California life with father, her silly brother, and her best friend, Lilly, who is in on her secret. But once Miley was cast, certain things about the show became clearer. In fact, Disney decided

The cast of *Hannah Montana*: (from left) Moises Arias (Rico), Jason Earles (Jackson Stewart), Billy Ray Cyrus (Robby Ray Stewart), Miley (Hannah Montana/Miley Stewart), Mitchel Musso (Oliver Oken), and Emily Osment (Lilly Truscott). Miley enjoyed working with the talented cast. She soon became particularly close friends with Emily and Mitchel.

Miley Cyrus flashes a peace sign backstage at a show. She and the other cast members worked on the show's first season during 2005. The actors filmed just 20 episodes of *Hannah Montana*. Disney would not order more episodes until it was sure that the show would be a hit.

to tailor its new show to its new starlet's own personal story. As writers began penning the first *Hannah Montana* episodes, bits of Miley's real life became part of the show. Billy Ray was now Robby Ray Stewart, a widowed songwriter who had made his name in country music. Miley became Miley Stewart, a southern girl transplanted to the West Coast.

Talented actors were cast in supporting roles on the show. Miley Stewart's older brother, Jackson, is a whiz at getting himself into sticky situations. After another long audition process, 29-year-old acting veteran Jason Earles was cast as Jackson. For Lilly, Miley's best friend, producers decided on Emily Osment. Eight months older than Miley, Emily proved to be a natural. Like Miley, she came from a show-business family. Her older brother, Haley Joel Osment, was nominated for an Oscar in 2000 for his role in the eerie **thriller** *The Sixth Sense*.

Now, with the central characters cast, *Hannah Montana* started production in early 2006. But there were challenges for the show's star. Although she was working far from her home in Tennessee, Miley still needed to get her education. With a full filming schedule, school was forced to compete with making the shows

CROSS-CURRENTS

If you want to know more about the actors on Hannah Montana, read "The Best Cast on Television." Go to page 53. ▶▶

and the publicity leading up to the first episode. Miley spoke about the back and forth that goes into making a television show when you are so young:

> **❝There's a tutor on the set, but it's difficult. I may act for 45 minutes, then do an hour of school and go back to acting. That makes it hard to concentrate on either acting or schooling. I hate math. I also hate history.❞**

What she did not hate was the work. As the **anticipation** grew and the premiere episode of *Hannah* approached, Miley could only hope that it all worked out. She had waited her whole life for this chance, sacrificing playtime to rehearse and practicing her singing while other kids kicked soccer balls. Both Miley and the Disney executives who had hired her hoped that she would now be able to connect with young fans.

Wearing her blonde wig, "Hannah" performs for an audience. *Hannah Montana* was an immediate hit—more than 5.4 million people watched the first episode, which aired on March 24, 2006. Both young viewers and their parents appreciated the show's underlying message: being true to who you really are is the only sure way to be truly happy.

The Birth of a Phenom

THE PREMISE OF *HANNAH MONTANA* SEEMS tailor-made for young girls: a pretty but otherwise average teenager leads a double life as a blonde-haired rock star. For audiences, there is something exciting in knowing the secret and watching others try to figure it out. But the show's premise was hardly a new one.

From at least the time of William Shakespeare in the 16th and 17th centuries—in plays such as *Twelfth Night* and *As You Like It*—writers have toyed with the idea of alter egos. In a famous scene from *As You Like It*, Shakespeare compared acting to real life:

> **"All the world's a stage,
> and all the men and women merely players:
> They have their exits and their entrances;
> And one man in his time plays many parts,
> his acts being seven ages."**

In the 20th century, comic-book writers and illustrators created superheroes: men and women with extraordinary powers who battled bad guys and saved the world from certain destruction over and over again. In a pinch, mild-mannered Clark Kent dashes into a phone booth, tears off his suit, and becomes Superman. Billionaire Bruce Wayne dons a mask and dark cowl to become Batman, the caped crusader. And the Amazon princess Diana, with her long black hair and red boots, is Wonder Woman.

Producers of *Hannah Montana* knew the long history but were intent on adding a fresh chapter. This time, a teen would live the secret life yet also have to deal with the trials and tribulations of growing up. Without any super powers or Shakespearean dialogue to help her, the character of Miley Stewart would struggle to balance her life of celebrity with her life as a sometimes mixed-up teenager.

⇒ GIVING IT A GO ⇐

The March 24, 2006, premiere of *Hannah Montana* was a gamble. New-fangled television shows always are. Importantly, the first episode established Miley's home life with her father Robby Ray and brother Jackson. But it also played on Miley's double life, as Lilly invites Miley to a Hannah Montana concert, not knowing her friend's secret identity.

While Disney executives believed they had a sure-fit hit, they boosted the show's chances by pairing it with a rebroadcast of the runaway hit *High School Musical*. It seemed like a no-brainer. After all, the hip and cheerful story of love, basketball, and the making of a high-school show was the most-watched film in the Disney Channel's 23-year history when it first aired in January 2006. The *Romeo and Juliet*–inspired television movie also **spawned** the best-selling album of that year, as well as truckloads of merchandise that hungry fans quickly gobbled up. It made sensations of dreamy Zac Efron, who played Troy, and charming Vanessa Hudgens as Gabriella.

Having curly-haired *High School* star Corbin Bleu guest star on the first *Hannah Montana* episode gave the new program a stamp of approval and a built-in audience that could only help. And help it did: More than 5.4 million people tuned in to watch the first *Hannah Montana* show—the Disney Channel's largest audience ever for a new program.

The news was good, very good, and Disney executives were over-the-moon excited about the prospects of *Hannah Montana*'s long-term success. When the second episode of the show also scored well in the ratings, Disney ordered six more episodes to be added to the already scheduled 20. They wanted more *Hannah Montana*, and they wanted it fast.

As for Miley and the cast, they seemed to know they were on the **cusp** of something big. Filming continued on *Hannah Montana* each day, and Miley was also responsible for helping to promote the show

A scene from the first season of *Hannah Montana*. During its first season, *Hannah* was the most popular show on television among viewers between the ages of six and 14. Disney soon ordered additional episodes of the program to be produced. The company also began to sell *Hannah Montana* clothing, dolls, and a CD of songs from the show.

on weekends. In June 2006 she performed as Hannah at Disney's Typhoon Lagoon in Walt Disney World in Orlando, Florida. She also went on a 39-city tour as the opening act for the Cheetah Girls, a popular Disney singing group. Miley and the show's cast also filmed a series of behind-the-scenes short takes called "Hannah Montana's Backstage Secrets." Other television tie-ins included Miley's guest spot in the movie *High School Musical 2*, in which she popped up at a pool party. For months, it seemed, Miley was everywhere Disney audiences were, and such promotion helped create a greater awareness of the show.

CROSS-CURRENTS

Often, when Miley tours her opening act is a band called the Jonas Brothers. To learn more about them, read "Brotherly Love." Go to page 54. ▶▶

In the end, the publicity paid off. In less than a year *Hannah Montana* was the number-one show on cable television. Among kids between the ages of six and 14, the program was the second most popular program on television, behind only *American Idol*. What began as a gamble was turning into a pop-culture **juggernaut**.

⇒ EXPANDING INTO NEW AREAS ⇐

But television was bound to become only one small part of Miley's entertainment empire. The *Hannah Montana* soundtrack, released on October 24, 2006, contained eight songs from the show, including "The Best of Both Worlds," "Just Like You," and "I Got Nerve." The album rocketed up the charts, selling millions of copies in just three short months. Cleverly, its cover even hinted at the secret of the show's success: Miley, dressed as Hannah, holds her forefinger to her lips, her eyes looking left. This nod and wink to Hannah's hush-hush real life only stoked interest in the show and the talented girl playing the pop princess.

Before long, too, Hannah Montana wigs, dolls, jewelry, handbags, and makeup flooded stores. On television, online, and in bedroom walls across the country, Hannah Montana fever was burning white-hot and bits of Hannah dialogue—such as "Sweet niblets!"—found their way into kids' everyday vocabulary.

Naturally, as Hannah Montana became a household name, more and more fans were eager to meet the perky teen beneath the golden locks. Who was Miley Cyrus, they wondered, and how had she gone from virtual unknown to Disney dynamo so quickly?

To help promote *Hannah Montana*, Disney offered Miley Cyrus a small role in the movie *High School Musical* 2. She had no lines in the film, just danced at the pool party near the end. *High School Musical* 2 was a huge hit—more than 17 million people tuned into the first showing, in August 2007.

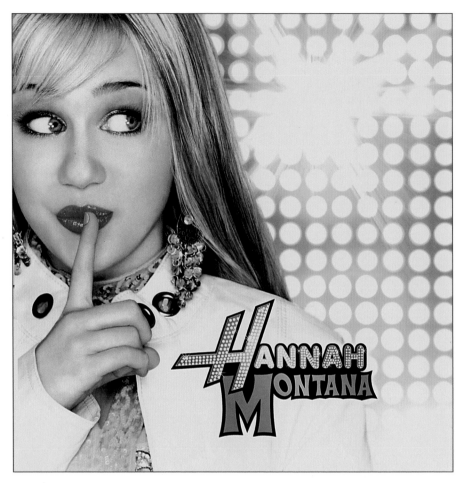

Miley, as Hannah, reminds fans to keep her secret on the cover of the *Hannah Montana* soundtrack album. She sang nine of the songs on the album, including a duet with her father. The *Hannah Montana* soundtrack was released in October 2006, and quickly became one of the year's best-selling albums.

NOT ALWAYS EASY

For Miley, her growing fame included many hard sacrifices. Thousands of miles from the rolling hills of her Tennessee farm, she missed her friends. Life had been simpler then, somehow, surrounded by her beloved dogs, cats, and horses. The bright spotlight was shining on her now, and its glare could often be harsh. Her every move was scrutinized, blogged about, and discussed on television and in teen magazines across the country.

Luckily, her close-knit family moved to Los Angeles with her, as they had moved to Toronto for Billy Ray years before. Although Disney was intent on transforming an ordinary country girl into a megastar, the Cyruses were just as **resolute** in their desire to

Miley poses with her father and actor Daniel Samonas on the *Hannah Montana* set. In the show's fourth episode, Samonas played Josh, a boy who invites Miley to attend a Hannah Montana concert with him. To protect her secret identity, Miley must try to be in two places at the same time.

provide Miley with as normal a home life as possible, something she deeply appreciates. She later said,

> **My family and I are very close. We fight back and forth just like all families, but I feel like I can tell my parents anything. When my dad and I come home from work, we forget that we work together and just hang out. We have a great relationship.**

Still, even family life is not without its more bizarre moments. For Miley, one of the strangest early episodes of the Hannah Montana rage took place in her own house. Unknown to Miley, her six-year-old sister Noah one day entered a Disney Channel contest. The prize: backstage passes to a Hannah Montana concert!

⇒ FRIENDS INDEED ⇐

The hectic schedule of studying her lines, shooting the show's second season, and doing her schoolwork did not leave much time for Miley's old friends from back home. But new friends were never far away. While spending long hours making *Hannah Montana*, Miley became good friends with her costars Emily Osment and Mitchel Musso, who plays schoolmate Oliver Oken on the show. To this day, the three are known to spend off hours sending each other text messages. They also place nighttime conference calls to gab and gossip with each other about the typical trials and tribulations of teenage life.

Then again, being a typical teenager is one thing. Keeping things in perspective despite the constant attention of fans and reporters is another. In her short time as a celebrity, Miley has discovered that fame brings many nice things: money, travel, and the ability to do what you want when you want to. At home, Miley even has her own separate apartment on the grounds of the family home. This gives her the privacy a young person often needs. Yet she spends her free time like so many others her age:

> **I really like just chilling with my friends and playing guitar. . . . I like to exercise, so I think that's fun to get all your energy out, because I've got a lot of energy all the time.**

Emily, Mitchel, and Miley have become close friends off the set of their hit show. A 2006 *New York Times* article reported, "In real life, Emily, Mitchel and Miley say they are constantly sending each other text messages offstage and gathering, at least electronically, in the evening for three-way conference calls in which they talk like the teenagers they are."

That energy is what keeps Miley going through television-show tapings, concerts, and public appearances like the 2008 Academy Awards. Decked out in a long and flowing fire-engine red dress, Miley walked the red carpet and waved to the thousands of fans who had waited all day to catch a glimpse of stars in their formal best. Yet somehow, despite the enormous attention, Miley has remained grounded and true to her down-home roots.

CROSS-CURRENTS

For some insights into why both adults and young people like Hannah Montana, read "Guest Stars." Go to page 55. ▶▶

MILEY CYRUS

Many stars have made guest appearances on *Hannah Montana*. For example, country music legend Dolly Parton (pictured here with Miley) has appeared several times as Miley Stewart's Aunt Dolly. (In real life, Dolly is actually Miley Cyrus's godmother.) Dolly later told reporters that being on the show exposed her to many new fans.

⇒ KEEPING IT REAL ⇐

Miley's friends and coworkers have noticed and admired the teenage star's uncanny ability to remain level-headed about fame and fortune while juggling a schedule that keeps her on the move constantly.

Although almost twice Miley's age, Jason Earles, who plays Hannah's zany brother, Jackson, has an abiding appreciation for Miley's ability to keep her crazy, exciting life in perspective. As a show-business veteran of movies such as 2004's *National Treasure* and the television show *The Shield*, Earles has watched as other actors, young and old, have let the **adulation** of fans go to their heads. But not Miley, as he says:

> **Miley really did come out of nowhere and suddenly became a sensation. . . . She's an adorable, energetic 14-year-old girl. But she's crazy, like every 14-year-old girl. She could be awful if she wanted to be. But she's not. She's about as sweet a person as you could want. . . . I think she understands how blessed we are. There's a million girls out there that would love to be her.**

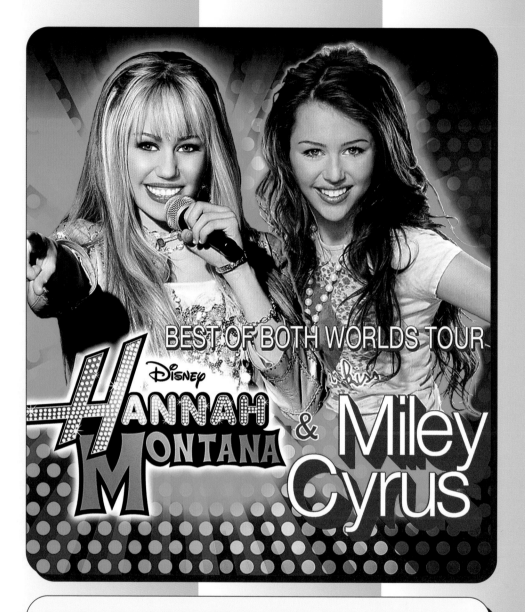

A poster for the Best of Both Worlds Tour, which began in October 2007 and ran through January 2008. Miley performed part of each show in character as Hannah, and the other half of the show as herself. She donated $1 from each ticket sold to benefit the City of Hope Foundation, which helps to fight cancer.

5

Both Worlds

SEASON TWO OF *HANNAH MONTANA* BEGAN WITH a bang. With one full season under their belts, the producers, writers, and actors were even more confident in their ongoing hit. Between seasons Miley Cyrus had grown and matured. She recorded an album and prepared for a concert tour that would take her across the country.

In its first season, *Hannah Montana* had been praised by both fans and TV critics. The show was even nominated for an Emmy Award for Outstanding Children's Program. The show also won a 2007 Teen Choice Award for Choice TV Show: Comedy.

In the second season, which began in April 2007, it was time for Miley Stewart to begin high school. The first episode of the season had her paired with pint-sized Rico, who claims to know Miley's secret. Miley has no choice but to act as if she is in love with him. In another episode, her boyfriend from season one, movie star Jake

Ryan, returns to Malibu looking to rekindle his romance with Miley. Fans, old and new, loved it.

By the fall of 2007, *Hannah Montana* had become a national sensation. Miley had already finished making the episodes for the second season. In October 2007, she began her Best of Both Worlds Tour. It was Miley's first concert tour as headliner, and expectations were growing by the day. Television ratings were still sky high, and record sales were through the roof. By now, Hannah Montana merchandise was hitting the stores, and Miley's face was gracing every teen publication cover imaginable, from *Girl's Life Magazine* to *Cosmo Girl*. Miley Cyrus, like her rock star **counterpart**, was a household name.

CROSS-CURRENTS

By 2007, Miley Cyrus was among the wealthiest young people in the country. To find out more, read "Youthful Moneymakers." Go to page 56. ▶▶

⟫ WE WANT MILEY! ⟪

The long lines and enormous demand for tickets to Miley's shows shocked the recording industry. Less than two years before, few people had heard of Miley Cyrus. Now she was contagious, traveling from city to city spreading a cheerful message of **empowerment** and innocent fun. Show sell-outs forced a tour extension, and the Best of Both Worlds Tour became one of the most successful concert tours of the year. In town after town, local radio stations held contests for Hannah tickets. News outlets covered the 15-year-old's every move. Some people were even willing to pay up to $2,500 just to get a glimpse of the young singer performing.

Not since the Beatles landed in New York City in 1964 had such an unbridled musical **mania** swept across the nation. But this was Hannah-mania, with fans building Web sites and posting their concert experiences, sharing pictures and videos from the concerts, and buying up every piece of merchandise they could find. Many fans, tykes and teens, even took to wearing blonde Hannah Montana wigs to the shows.

CROSS-CURRENTS

If you want to learn more about the rigors of a concert tour, read "Miley on the Road." Go to page 57. ▶▶

Yet the Hannah Montana craze does not always bring out the best in people. In late December 2007 a Dallas, Texas, store named Club Libby Lu awarded a six-year-old girl four tickets to a Hannah Montana concert, as well as other prizes, based on an essay she wrote. The child began her essay by saying that her father, a soldier, had recently died in Iraq. But

By April 2007, when this issue of *CosmoGirl* magazine appeared, Miley had become the hottest young star on television. She appeared on many magazine covers, and was in high demand for interviews. Miley's young fans eagerly purchased her albums, as well as backpacks, T-shirts, dolls, and other items carrying the name Hannah Montana.

when the U.S. Department of Defense claimed to have no record of the soldier's death, the little girl's mother admitted she had lied. On a local television news show, Priscilla Ceballos claimed they did what they had to in order to win. Consequently, Club Libby Lu, which sells girls clothes and accessories, withdrew the prize and gave it to another contestant. It was a rare, unpleasant chapter in an otherwise sunny storm of pop-culture madness.

When Miley arrived at the world premiere of the 3-D movie *Hannah Montana and Miley Cyrus: Best of Both World Concert* in January 2008, she was not surprised to find celebrity photographers lining the red carpet. It was something of a shock to see that the photographers were wearing blonde Hannah wigs, however!

⇒ THE SHOW THAT NEVER ENDS ⇐

For all the joy and **exhilaration** fame brings, one aspect of being in the public eye that Miley is less comfortable with are the many rumors spread about her. Fans hungry for any tidbits of information about their idol's private life go online and read teen magazines, trolling for any news or gossip about her. For example, after Nick Jonas, the curly-haired singer in the boy band Jonas Brothers, was seen out on the town with Miley, rumors spread that they were dating. Miley has said that such intrusions into her private life cause her heartache and pain.

Expectations are high for Miley to be a role model for her young fans. She gladly accepts the responsibility. In an interview with *Entertainment Tonight*, Miley spoke about the importance of always trying to do the right things:

> **"I don't want to be perfect, but I do want to be a role model. My mom always tells me that imperfections equal beauty. All of us are imperfect. "**

Confetti drops on screaming fans as Hannah performs a song during a concert. The Best of Both Worlds Tour was one of the hottest tickets of late 2007 and early 2008. Even though Miley only toured for the last two-and-a-half months of 2007, her sold-out tour still ranked among the top-earning tours of the year.

➢ SEATBELT CONTROVERSY ➣

Another controversy was fueled when the movie *Hannah Montana and Miley Cyrus: Best of Both Worlds Concert* was released in February 2008. The watchdog magazine *Consumer Reports*, as well as many moviegoers, noticed that during one scene in which Miley and Billy Ray Cyrus ride in a Range Rover to a tour rehearsal, the young star does not wear a seatbelt. In most states, driving without a seat belt is illegal. Billy Ray was quick to respond to the issue:

> **"We got caught up in the moment of filming, and we made a mistake and forgot to buckle our seat belts. Seat belt safety is extremely important."**

Around the time of the fastening **faux pas**, Disney was criticized too. It released the Miley/Hannah concert movie by proclaiming that its theatrical run would only be one week long. Because of the overwhelming demand for the limited supply of tickets, a frenzy soon began. Kids screamed for tickets; moms and dads rushed to purchase them before they were scooped up. The excitement translated to big numbers at the box office. During its first weekend, *Hannah Montana and Miley Cyrus: Best of Both Worlds Concert* earned $31 million in sales. The movie broke the record for a movie opening during Super Bowl weekend. Yet despite the original announcement, the movie's run was not limited at all. Instead, *Best of Both Worlds Concert* continued running for weeks in theaters. Had Disney honestly planned to screen the movie for only seven days? Or did the company use the marketing plan to increase publicity and demand for the film?

➢ "WE GOT THE PARTY" ➣

In January 2008 Miley made a major life change. Citing the fact that family and friends had always referred to her by her nickname, the star legally changed her name from Destiny Hope Cyrus to Miley Ray Cyrus, as a tribute to her father.

Like the official name change, the release of *Hannah Montana and Miley Cyrus: Best of Both Worlds Concert* in February 2008 seemed to mark a new beginning for the pop star. Fans flocked to see the film. Donning dark 3-D glasses, moviegoers could experience Miley up close and personal.

The propulsive sound of a rhythm guitar cuts through the darkened arena. Shimmering lights, like stars, flash on the stage. The screams of thousands of high-pitched voices shatter the relative calm. "Are you ready for Hannah Montana?!" a voice asks. Then she appears, dancing up a storm, descending from above in a large, transparent, purple-colored box. Is it really her? Once she begins singing there is no doubt. The rock star has arrived. Hannah Montana bursts forward, rushing along the thin strip of stage that extends into the audience. Hands reach out to grab her. Microphone in one hand, she touches as many of them as she can.

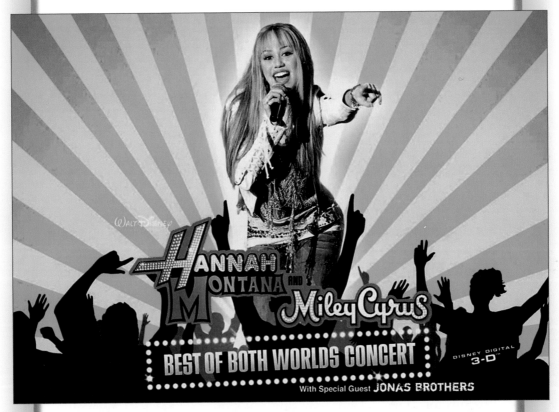

A poster for the 3-D film *Hannah Montana and Miley Cyrus: Best of Both World Concert*, which was released in the United States in February 2008. Two of Miley's early shows on the tour were filmed to create the movie. The film has been released in several other countries, including Mexico, the United Kingdom, Australia, Germany, and Brazil.

Superstardom came quickly for Miley Cyrus, but she is not ready to simply sit back and enjoy her accomplishments. In July Miley's album *Breakout* was released. She has also been working on a full-length *Hannah Montana* movie, as well as a book about her life. Both the movie and book are scheduled to be released in 2009.

For the next 40 minutes, Hannah reigns supreme, belting out live versions of "Bigger than Us" and "Nobody's Perfect." Only after bringing out the Jonas Brothers for a version of "We Got the Party" does Hannah do a disappearing act. The boys pick up the slack with renditions of "When You Look Me in the Eyes" and "Year 3000."

When the teen queen returns, it is as Miley, singing "Start All Over." Blonde wig gone, her secret identity revealed for the adoring crowd, Miley Cyrus seems content just being herself and showing her many fans the real her.

⇒ A SPECIAL TRIBUTE ⇐

Perhaps the most heartfelt moment of each evening's show is when Miley sits barefoot on a stool, a guitar propped upon her knee, and begins strumming the chords to a song she wrote. Most of the songs played on *Hannah Montana* or sung by its star are written by others. Yet "I Miss You" is different. Cowritten by Brian Green, Wendi Foy Green, and Miley, the song is a tribute.

The song was first heard during season one of *Hannah Montana*. In the episode "She's a Super Sneak," Miley Stewart sings the chorus of the song as an homage to her late mother. In reality, the song was written for Miley's grandfather, Ron Cyrus, who died in early 2006.

As part of the concert, it provides a moment of reflection:

"I miss you/I miss your smile/And I still shed a tear/ Every once in a while/And even though it's different now/You're still here somewhere/My heart won't let you go/And I need you to know/I miss you."

Hands in the air, the crowd sways to the easy beat of the sad but sweet song. But they are not in their seats for long. As the song ends, the music throbs and Miley sings her signature song, "The Best of Both Worlds." It is an appropriate song to end on because, after years of reaching for the top, Miley Cyrus has made it.

⇒ "START ALL OVER" ⇐

Miley Cyrus has come a long way to achieve stardom. She has traveled thousands of miles, leaving the comfort of her home in hopes of making a splash. In less than two years that splash has become a tidal wave. She retains the Tennessee twang and still calls herself a country girl at heart, but Miley is also a rock star with millions of fans who want to dress like her, sound like her, and be like her. She lives in both worlds and somehow manages to make it work.

For many, Miley's ability to balance the two halves of her life is an inspiration. Fans are eager to see what she does next. Miley's success also serves a higher purpose by giving hope to all those young girls who dream of reaching for the stars.

Extreme Miley: A Chance to Give Back

Despite her busy schedule, Miley makes a great effort to give back to her fans. A recent episode of the hit television show *Extreme Makeover: Home Edition* told the story of Sergeant Daniel Gilyeat, a marine who lost his leg in 2005 while serving in the Iraq War. A single father of four children, Gilyeat struggled to shelter his family in a small, run-down house. While the show built the family a new house from scratch, Gilyeat and his kids were treated to a Hannah Montana concert. Best of all, Miley herself welcomed 9-year-old Alexis and her sister and two brothers backstage after the show.

Such good works are typical for the star. Other recent good works include an appearance for St. Jude's Children's Hospital in Memphis, Tennessee, and *American Idol*'s highly successful charitable broadcast "Idol Gives Back," along with other musical artists such as Bono, John Legend, and Mariah Carey. Before a recent sold-out concert in the City of Brotherly Love, Miley modeled and then auctioned off a personalized team jersey given to her by the National

"One of the main reasons my family and I support St. Jude is because there is always something you can do for someone else," Miley Cyrus said about participating in an event to benefit the internationally famous research hospital. *"It is great to be able to encourage kids to learn and help other kids at the same time."*

Basketball Association's Philadelphia 76ers Proceeds from the sale went to local Philadelphia organizations. When in need, Miley is a friend indeed. (Go back to page 6.)

Reaching Out: Miley in 3-D

The *Hannah Montana and Miley Cyrus: Best of Both Worlds Concert* is not the first three-dimensional (3-D) movie. In fact, the technique was pioneered in the late 1890s. To make a 3-D movie, two cameras are typically positioned facing one another at a 90 degree angle, using mirrors. When the film is shown, the human eye is tricked into believing that images on the screen are popping out.

A poster for It Came From Outer Space, *one of many 3-D movies released during the early 1950s. During the early 1950s, 3-D films were extremely popular, with studios releasing dozens of 3-D movies. The 3-D craze ended by 1955, however, and since then very few movies have been released in that format.*

The first use of 3-D glasses to enhance the viewing experience was for the 1922 film *The Power of Love*. But until the 1952 release of *Bwana Devil*, a jungle adventure about a couple of man-eating lions, and 1953's horror-fest *House of Wax*, 3-D movies remained little more than novelties.

Although the technique was virtually forgotten in the 1970s and 1980s, the last decade has brought 3-D movies back with a cinematic vengeance—especially when combined with enormous IMAX projection theaters. The 3-D feature in the Hannah movie is a perfect way to experience the concert up close. For a star who loves her fans as much Miley does, 3-D technology lets her reach out and almost touch them. (Go back to page 9.) ◀◀

Achy-Breaky Pop

Superstardom runs in the Cyrus family. Long before the Hannah Montana craze, right around the time Tish was giving birth to Miley, Billy Ray Cyrus was burning up the country music charts.

Miley and her dad Billy Ray Cyrus pose on the cover of the April 2008 Cowboys and Indians *magazine. Billy Ray rocketed to country music superstardom in the early 1990s, when his single "Achy Breaky Heart" became a smash hit. Since then, Billy Ray has had seven other top-10 hits on the country music charts.*

Born in Flatwoods, Kentucky, in 1961, Billy Ray's first love was baseball, not music. As a teen he won an athletic scholarship to Georgetown College, located near his home. Yet music was always there, competing for his attention. It was about this time that Cyrus dropped his dreams of playing major league ball and picked up a guitar instead.

After years of hard work, playing small clubs and honing his skills as a songwriter, he finally struck it big with his 1992 album *Some Gave All*. Although the record eventually sold 9 million copies, it was the single "Achy Breaky Heart" that catapulted the 31-year-old to mainstream success. The bouncy song was catchy and fun. For many women, though, it was the video they remembered. With his chiseled features and stylish mullet, Billy Ray Cyrus became country's newest heartthrob. "Achy Breaky Heart" shot to the top of the charts and went on to win Single of the Year at the Country Music Awards. (Go back to page 11.) ◀◀

The Home of Country Music

A group of musicians perform at the famous Grand Ole Opry House, a 4,400-seat theater near Nashville, Tennessee. Many of country music's greatest performers have appeared at the Opry over the years, including such modern stars as Garth Brooks, Reba McEntire, Carrie Underwood, Clint Black, Trisha Yearwood, and Trace Adkins.

Nashville, where Miley Cyrus was raised, is the state capital of Tennessee. Founded in 1779 and named for Revolutionary War hero Francis Nash, the city is also the spiritual home of American country music. Aside from hosting the annual Country Music Awards Music Festival, which draws thousands of fans, Nashville is also the site of the Country Music Hall of Fame.

Nashville's most famous musical fixture is the Grand Ole Opry. Started in 1925, the Opry is the longest-running radio show in the nation. Broadcast locally on WSM every Friday and Saturday night, the homespun, music-centered program has helped launch the careers of such legendary performers as Willie Nelson, Patsy Cline, George Jones, and Dolly Parton. In 1954 the Opry saw the one and only appearance of the future "King of Rock and Roll," Elvis Presley. The newcomer's gyrations and loud music prevented a return invitation. Over the years, the Opry branched out: the Opryland theme park entertained patrons from 1972 to 1997 but has since been replaced by the Opry Mills mega-mall. Yet one thing that has not changed is the Opry's dedication to American country music. (Go back to page 13.)

Disney's Star Machine: Hayley Mills and Annette Funicello

Miley Cyrus is only the latest in a string of Disney performers who have captured the imaginations of teens around the world. At 14, British actress Hayley Mills was signed by Walt Disney himself to a five-year movie contract. Her first Disney film, 1960's bright and cheery *Pollyanna*, was a critical and popular success. And over the next half decade, the hits just kept coming. The high-point of Mills's Disney career is, perhaps, her roles as twin sisters in the classic *The Parent Trap*. With her blond hair, bright smile, and winning attitude, Mills the Brit became America's little sweetheart.

The *Parent Trap* soundtrack, including the title song, was sung by Disney's other "It" girl, the dark-haired beauty Annette Funicello. Having gotten her start on the original *Mickey Mouse Club* television show in the early 1950s, Funicello soon grew into a popular big-screen attraction. She appeared in Disney movies and television shows, and also had several hit songs during the late 1950s and early 1960s. Eventually, she moved on from Disney and starred with singer Frankie Avalon in a series of California surf movies, including *Beach Party* and *Beach*

As one of the original Mouseketeers on the 1950s television show Mickey Mouse Club, *Annette Funicello was so popular that she received thousands of fan letters each month. She went on to star in many Disney movies during the 1950s and early 1960s. Annette also had a successful singing career recording several hits for Disney.*

Blanket Bingo. Although Funicello's shapely figure made her extremely popular among boys, she retained a wholesome image on and off screen. (Go back to page 20.)

The Best Cast on Television

While some critics have called them the best cast on television, the actors who make *Hannah Montana* call it all a day's work. Whether it is Jackson trying to get one over on dear old dad, as he did when he went out to play volleyball without his sunscreen; or pint-sized Rico (played by Moises Arias) looking to hire a buff version of himself for a television advertisement, each member of the ensemble brings his or her own unique qualities. Onscreen chemistry is not a given, yet Miley and her fellow actors seem to have it down to a science.

Most telling is the connection Miley has with Emily Osment, who also plays dual roles, both as Miley's best friend, Lilly, and Hannah's best friend, Lola. Writers have drawn on the rich history of classic television comedy teams such as Ralph Cramden and Ed Norton and Abbott and Costello to pepper the situations they put the two girls in. The most common comparison, though, is that of Lucille Ball and Vivian Vance, who became known as the greatest female comedy team in television history for their work on the groundbreaking sitcom *I Love Lucy*. (Go back to page 25.)

The cast of Hannah Montana *(from left, Emily Osment, Miley Cyrus, Jason Earles, Billy Ray Cyrus, and Mitchel Musso) have been praised for the way in which they work together and complement each other. Some television critics have compared Miley to Lucille Ball, one of the greatest comics in TV history.*

◀◀

Brotherly Love

The Jonas Brothers, often the opening act for Hannah Montana on tour, are already veterans of the music business. Nick Jonas began performing on Broadway at the tender age of seven in shows such as *Beauty and the Beast* and *Les Miserables*. By 2005 Nick and his brothers Joe and Kevin were writing songs and touring in support of acts such as Jesse McCartney and Kelly Clarkson. Their first album, *It's About Time*, only reached number 91 on the Billboard charts, but their second, *The Jonas Brothers*, released in August 2007, peaked at number 5. Their appearance on *Hannah Montana*, in an episode titled "Me and Mr. Jonas and Mr. Jonas and Mr. Jonas," brought them more notoriety. It also brought them closer to Miley herself, so their work on her 2007 tour made perfect sense.

In 2008, the Jonas Brothers—Kevin, Joe, and Nick Jonas—released their third album, A Little Bit Longer. *During 2007, the brothers guest-starred on an episode of* Hannah Montana. *They later joined Miley Cyrus on the road, performing as the opening act at most stops on her sold-out Best of Both Worlds concert tour.*

Since then, the Jonas Brothers have worked to break out of the teen-scene mold. In March 2008, the brothers lit up the popular television show *Dancing with the Stars* with a rocking version of the 1980s mega-hit "Take on Me" by the Norwegian band A-Ha.

(Go back to page 30.) ◀◀

Guest Stars

Kids love *Hannah Montana* because a regular teenage girl gets to moonlight as a sensational and popular rock star. Parents like the show because of Hannah's strong values and the chance to watch some of the favorite stars of their generation mix it up with Miley, Billy Ray, and the rest of the award-winning cast. The massive popularity of the show has made it easy to attract some of the bigger names in the entertainment industry to appear on the show.

Recent guests include some of the most popular stars of yesterday and today. In a recent episode, Dwayne "the Rock" Johnson, star of the family hit *The Game Plan*, played himself. Miley and Lilly tricked him into a girly makeover. Country music legend Dolly Parton, as Miley's aunt, likes to mix it up with Miley's grandmother, played by Vicki Lawrence. Most unusual was the guest shot of Larry David, star of HBO's *Curb Your Enthusiasm*. In the episode, David is frustrated because he can't get a table in a restaurant. His two real-life daughters stand starstruck as Hannah walks by and gets exactly what she wants. (Go back to page 35.) ◀◀

Lilly and Miley give professional wrestler Dwayne "The Rock" Johnson a makeover in an attempt to get an embarrassing picture of him in one notable Hannah Montana *episode. Other celebrities who have appeared on the show include Dolly Parton, Brooke Shields (as Miley's mother, Susan Stewart), Heather Locklear (as Lilly's mom), and High Schoo*

Youthful Moneymakers

The year 2007 was a lucrative one for teen sensation Miley Cyrus. Aside from her television show, Miley earned big bucks from the *Hannah Montana* soundtrack; the release of her hit double album, *Hannah Montana 2: Meet Miley Cyrus*; and the 2007 kickoff o her concert tour. Overall, *Forbes* magazine reported that she earned about $3.5 millior for the year. In *Forbes*'s annual list o top-earning superstars under the age o 25, Miley comes in a number 17.

Many of the people on the Forbes list are athletes, such as basketbal superstars LeBron Jame ($27 million) and Carmelo Anthony ($10 million) football player Reggie Bush ($24 million), tenni star Maria Sharapova ($23 million), and gol phenomenon Michell Wie ($19 million). Othe actors ahead of Miley on the list include *Harry Potter* stars Daniel Rad cliffe ($15 million), Ruper Grint, and Emma Watson ($4 million each). Forme Disney star Hilary Duf ranked seventh overal earning $12 million. Othe stars on the list wit Disney connections include Keira Knightley ($9 million) Dakota Fanning ($4 million Lindsay Lohan ($3.5 mi lion), and Frankie Muni ($3 million). (Go back t

YOUNG MONEY
your life. right now.

An InCharge Publication
MAR/APRIL 2006
$3.95
www.youngmoney.com

STUDENT INVESTING ADVICE

COLLEGE CAR CLUBS

Hilary Duff
Young and Powerful
America's teen idol talks about her career, entrepreneurship and personal sacrifices

+ TECH Gadget Guide

4 CAN'T-MISS JOB HUNTING TIPS

Hilary Duff, featured here on a magazine cover from 2006, is one of the top-earning young people today. Hilary owes much of her success as an actress and pop singer to her work on the Disney Channel series Lizzie McGuire. Miley has said that she admires

Miley on the Road

Because she used to travel with her father during the days that he was a country music superstar, Miley is no stranger to tour buses. During the Best of Both Worlds tour, which ran from mid-October to the end of January, Miley traveled on a luxury bus with her family. Here, Miley opens a DVD player on the bus.

Traveling to dozens of different cities in only a matter of weeks, eating on the run, and sleeping when you can is bound to take a toll on even the most road-savvy entertainer. Luckily for Miley, she travels with her mom and dad and some of her siblings on a luxury bus that serves as their home away from home. Loaded with electronic gadgets—televisions, iPods, and computer equipment—the bus provides all the comforts of home, and then some.

When it is time for shut-eye, Miley climbs into one of the bunks and snuggles up with her Elvis Presley blanket and a picture of her beloved grandfather close by. On days when she is not performing, she and her show dancers make their way to local clothing stores and try on the latest fashions. For Miley, the goal is trying to live as normal a life as possible, even when she is constantly moving from place to place. It sure helps that Tish Cyrus is along, not just for the ride, but to help Miley change from Hannah Montana into her real self during the show.

(Go back to page 40.)

1992 Destiny Hope Cyrus is born on November 23 near Nashville, Tennessee.

2002 The Cyrus family moves to Toronto, Canada, when Billy Ray Cyrus is cast in the television show *Doc*.

That same year, 10-year-old Destiny, now known as Miley, is cast in a small part.

2003 Miley is noticed by famed film director Tim Burton and is cast as young Ruthie in Burton's movie *Big Fish*.

2004 During the final year of *Doc*'s production, Miley is again called on to appear on the show, this time in a larger role.

Miley is also seen as the spokesperson for Daisy Rock Guitars.

She sends in an audition tape to Disney but is considered too small.

2005 Miley auditions for Disney and is cast in the role of Hannah Montana.

The Cyrus family moves to Los Angeles from Franklin, Tennessee, in December.

2006 *Hannah Montana* premieres on March 24 as a lead-in to a broadcast of *High School Musical*. The show draws 5.4 million viewers that first night.

2007 Season two of *Hannah Montana* begins on April 23; by now, the show is the highest-rated program on cable television.

Miley begins a nationwide concert tour.

2008 In January, Miley legally changes her name from Destiny Hope Cyrus to Miley Ray Cyrus.

The movie *Hannah Montana and Miley Cyrus: Best of Both Worlds Concert* is released for one week, from February 1 through 7; demand is overwhelming and the run of the film is extended; in its first weekend of release, the movie earns $31 million at the box office.

In April, Miley and Billy Ray Cyrus host CMT Music Awards.

2009 *Miles to Go*, the first book by Miley Cyrus, reaches number one on the *New York Times* children's best seller list.

In April, *Hannah Montana: The Movie* is released.

Hit Singles

2007 "Ready, Set, Don't Go" (Billy Ray Cyrus featuring Miley Cyrus)
"See You Again"
"G.N.O." (Girl's Night Out)
"I Miss You"
"Start All Over"
"Life's What You Make It"
"Nobody's Perfect"

2008 "Rock Star"
"7 Things"

Albums

2006 *Hannah Montana*

2007 *Hannah Montana 2: Meet Miley Cyrus*

2008 *Hannah Montana and Miley Cyrus: Best of Both Worlds Concert*
Breakout

Awards

2006–2007 Golden Icon Awards, "Best Child Role Model,"

2007 *Popstar* magazine, "Poptastic Queen"
Teen Choice Awards, "Choice TV Actress: Comedy" for *Hannah Montana*
Teen Choice Awards, "Choice Summer Artist"
Kids' Choice Awards, "Favorite Television Actress" for *Hannah Montana*

2008 Kids' Choice Awards, "Favorite Female Singer"
Kids' Choice Awards, "Favorite Television Actress" for *Hannah Montana*
Young Artist Awards, "Best Performance in a TV Series as a Leading
Young Actress."

Books

Alexander, Lauren. *Mad for Miley: An Unauthorized Biography*. New York: Price Stern Sloan, 2007.

Cyrus, Billy Ray. *The Other Side*. Nashville: Word Music, 2003.

Gabler, Neal. *Walt Disney: The Triumph of the American Imagination*. New York: Vintage, 2007.

Robb, Jackie. *Miley Mania: Miley Cyrus Unauthorized*. New York: Scholastic, 2008.

Web Sites

http://www.disney.go.com

Since it brought us Miley and Hannah, a stop at the "official home page of all things Disney" is a must. Click on the television tab and find Hannah and Jackson. For new fans of the show, the "Characters" feature will bring you up to speed on the storyline and important players. Before you go, play a few Hannah-related games or download a buddy icon for chat-room fun.

http://www.mileycyrus.com

This is the official stop for all things Miley. You can listen to her music, catch up on the latest Miley news—including tour information—and watch behind-the-scenes videos. This wholesome, "all-about-you" site is also your ticket to Miley World, where you can have fun chatting with other fans, buying advance concert tickets, and participating in a variety of Miley-oriented contests.

http://www.mileycyrusheaven.com

Another fan site, this one is a bit more low key, but it contains just about everything you will need to worship the pop princess, including links to Miley ringtones, a growing list of Miley quotes, and a heaping helping of award-show video footage of Miley in action.

http://www.mileyfans.net

Want to learn some Miley and Hannah lyrics so you can "wow" friends and family? Check out this cluttered but well-organized shrine to America's reigning teen queen. Download Miley calendars, computer wallpaper, and photographs, or read tour stories from fellow fans like Nina and Penny, who laugh, cry, and scream at the top of their lungs for their idol whenever they get the chance.

adulation—flattery or admiration.

ambition—a strong feeling of wanting to be successful in life and achieve great things.

anticipation—the feeling of looking forward, usually excitedly or eagerly, to something that is going to happen.

audition—a test in the form of a short performance; a tryout.

brood—one's family or offspring.

counterpart—somebody or something that resembles another or functions similarly.

critics—people who judge somebody or something.

cusp—the borderline between things.

empowerment—to give somebody power or authority.

exhilaration—the joy, happiness, and/or excitement that celebrity brings.

faux pas—French for an embarrassing mistake.

gene—the basic unit capable of transmitting characteristics from one generation to the next. It consists of a specific sequence of DNA or RNA that occupies a fixed position locus on a chromosome.

hunch—an intuitive feeling about something.

illustrator—a person who draws.

jaded—tired or bored .

juggernaut—an overwhelming force.

legions—large numbers of people.

limelight—the focus of attention or public interest.

mania—an excessive and intense interest in or enthusiasm for something.

resolute—possessing determination and purposefulness.

résumé—a list of work experiences and achievements, typically presented to a potential employer.

spawned—a seed, germ, or the source of something.

spokesperson—somebody authorized to speak on behalf of another person or other people.

three-dimensional—possessing or appearing to possess the dimensions of height, width, and depth.

thriller—a book, play, or movie that has an exciting plot involving crime and mystery.

throngs—crowds of people.

page 5 "I could fix the flat . . ." Miley Cyrus, "Rock Star." *Hannah Montana 2: Meet Miley Cyrus* (2007).

page 6 "We rocked out to every . . ." Miley Fans, "Meghan and Brooke's Story." (March 16, 2008). http://mileyfans.net/tour_stories.php.

page 9 "I've always loved singing . . ." Ann Oldenburg, "Miley Cyrus Fulfills Her Destiny." *USA Today* (January 14, 2007). http://www.usatoday.com/life/television/news/2007-01-10-miley-cyrus_x.htm.

page 12 "When I was little . . ." Oldenburg, "Miley Cyrus Fulfills Her Destiny."

page 15 "Since she was little . . ." Oldenburg, "Miley Cyrus Fulfills Her Destiny."

page 21 "We saw a girl . . ." Ann Oldenburg, "Lifelong Work Pays Off, Says Miley Cyrus, 13." *USA Today* (March 23, 2006). http://www.usatoday.com/life/television/news/2006-03-23-miley-cyrus_x.htm.

page 21 "As I read the script . . ." Audrey T. Hingley, "Hosanna, Montana!" *Today's Christian* (January/February 2008). http://www.christianitytoday.com/tc/2008/001/1.19.html.

page 22 "I didn't know . . ." Jacques Steinberg, "Hannah Montana and Miley Cyrus: A Tale of Two Tweens." *New York Times* (April 20, 2006). http://www.nytimes.com/2006/04/20/arts/television/20cyru.html?_r=1&scp=1&sq=jacques+steinberg+hannah+montana+and+miley+cyrus+a+tale+of+two+tweens&st=nyt&oref=slogin.

page 25 "There's a tutor . . ." James Brady, "In Step with Miley Cyrus." *Parade* (February 4, 2007): http://www.parade.com/articles/editions/2007/edition_02-04-2007/In-Step-With-Miley-Cyrus

page 27 "All the world's a stage . . ." William Shakespeare, *Twelfth Night* (Boston: Allyn and Bacon, 1922), p. 39.

page 34 "My family and I . . ." Hingley, "Hosanna, Montana!"

page 34 "I really like just chilling . . ." CBBC Newsround, "Hotseat: Hannah Montana." (March 28, 2007). http://news.bbc.co.uk/cbbcnews/hi/newsid_6480000/newsid_6484900/6484997.stm.

page 35 "In real life . . ." Steinberg, "Hannah Montana and Miley Cyrus: A Tale of Two Teens."

page 37 "Miley really did come out . . ." Oldenburg, "Miley Cyrus Fulfills Her Destiny."

page 43 "I don't want to be . . ." Tirdad Derakhshani, "Miley's Confessional." *Philadelphia Inquirer* (January 20, 2008), p. B2.

page 44 "We got caught up . . ." Fox News, "Billy Ray Cyrus Says He, Miley Just Forgot to Buckle Up." (February 13, 2008). http://www.foxnews.com/story/0,2933,330634,00.html.

page 47 "I miss you . . ." Miley Cyrus, "I Miss You." *Hannah Montana 2: Meet Miley Cyrus* (2007).

page 48 "One of the main . . ." Miley Cyrus, quoted in a St. Jude Children's Hospital press release. (November 5, 2007). http://www.stjude.org/stjude/v/index.jsp?vgnextoid=c4baf7fc09016110VgnVCM1000001e0215acRCRD&vgnextchannel=9f6113c016118010VgnVCM1000000e2015acRCRD

Numbers in **bold italics** refer to captions.

David Robson is an award-winning writer and English professor. He is the recipient of a National Endowment for the Arts grant and two playwriting fellowships from the Delaware Division of the Arts. He dedicates this book to his daughter, Ingrid, who considers herself Miley Cyrus and Hannah Montana's number-one fan. Robson lives with his family in Wilmington, Delaware.

PICTURE CREDITS

page

1: Getty Images

4: Disney Channel/NMI

7: Disney Channel/NMI

8: Russell Einhorn/Splash Photos

10: Miley-Cyrus.com/CIC Photos

13: Miley-Cyrus.com/CIC Photos

14: Miley-Cyrus.com/CIC Photos

16: CMA/PRMS

19: Walt Disney World/PRMS

20: Time & Life Pictures/Getty Images

22: Disney Channel/NMI

23: Disney Channel/NMI

24: Getty Images for Distinctive Assets

26: Disney Channel/NMI

29: Disney Channel/NMI

31: Walt Disney Pictures/NMI

32: Walt Disney Records/NMI

33: Disney Channel/NMI

35: Disney Channel/NMI

36: Disney Channel/NMI

38: Walt Disney Pictures/NMI

41: COSMO/NMI

42: Kevin Winter/Getty Images

43: Splash Photos

45: Walt Disney Pictures/NMI

46: Disney Channel/NMI

48: St. Jude Children's Hospital/PRMS

49: Universal International Pictures/NMI

50: Cowboys Indians/NMI

51: T&T/IOA Photos

52: Boomers Pinups/CHA

53: Disney Channel/NMI

54: Gerardo Mora/Getty Images

55: Disney Channel/NMI

56: Young Money/NMI

57: Startraks Photo/CIC Photos

Front cover: Kevin Parry/WireImage